Made in the USA
Monee, IL
20 May 2022

96812535R00075